Beauty & Grace

90-DAY DEVOTIONAL

BroadStreet
PUBLISHING

BroadStreet Publishing Group LLC
Racine, Wisconsin, USA
Broadstreetpublishing.com

Beauty & Grace: 90-Day Devotional

978-1-4245-5665-6

Devotional entries compiled by Michelle Winger.

Design by Chris Garborg | garborgdesign.com
Edited by Michelle Winger | literallyprecise.com

Printed in China.

18 19 20 21 22 23 24   7 6 5 4 3 2 1

I praise you because I am

fearfully and wonderfully made;

your works are wonderful,

I know that full well.

PSALM 139:14 NIV

Introduction

We know from Scripture that the unfading beauty of a gentle and quiet spirit is of great worth in God's sight. But how do we find quiet in a busy world, and embrace this definition of beauty that is not at all popular?

This 90-day devotional will encourage you to spend time with God, experiencing his peace and joy, and being refreshed in his presence. Let anxiety melt away, and be filled with the confidence of knowing your Creator cherishes you because he made you.

Walk in the beauty and grace that God has purposed for you.

> *I remain confident of this:*
> *I will see the goodness of the LORD*
> *in the land of the living.*
> PSALM 27:13 NIV

There is nothing more reassuring than the confident hope that comes from God. A knowledge that what is coming is better than what is. We all come against many difficulties in our lives, but hearing that it's all going to be okay can be the difference between getting through it and giving up.

I will remain confident. What a beautiful promise to speak out when you're in the hardest of times. Better things are coming. You can be assured there are blessings for you. That you will see, firsthand, the goodness of a loving God in the land of living—the really living. Not just getting by, or barely getting through, but being truly alive.

Those who have tasted and seen know that God is good.

> *Do you know the goodness of God?*
> *How have you seen his goodness*
> *in your life recently?*

Thank you, God, that you are good.
Thank you that you have promised your
goodness and your faithfulness to me—
and that no matter how hard things get,
I can be confident that I will see you
and be alive with you.

Who will show us some good?
Lift up the light of your face upon us, O Lord.
You have put more joy in my heart
than they have when their grain and wine abound.
PSALM 4:6-7 ESV

The clearing of the land broke all the soft skin on
your hand that had never labored like that before.
The dropping and covering of each seed in the dirt
was done with a whispered prayer of hope. When
the rain did not fall, you pleaded. When it came, you
breathed a sigh of relief. When it raised too high,
you held your breath. Each day a prayer was on your
every breath—these crops were your life.

You partnered with God to bring life, but ultimately
it was out of your control. The heat came, and
what was tiny grew large. The air cooled, the mood
shifted, and the time had finally come: harvest. There
was goodness to be collected and joy to be found in
all that hope: bubbling over like a cup of new wine.

We find joy in life knowing our hope has been fulfilled in Christ. Our joy is founded on that unshakeable truth.

Are you excited for a season of fulfilled hope?

Thank you, Jesus, for restoring my hope. Thank you for being with me during the season of labor and toil. I look forward to seeing your goodness played out in my life.

*Let your adorning be the hidden person of the heart
with the imperishable beauty of a gentle and quiet
spirit, which in God's sight is very precious.*
1 PETER 3:4 ESV

Beauty is a powerful influencer in the lives of women. We are constantly bombarded with images and messages of what beauty is and what it should be. Even if we are confident in who we are, it can still be difficult not to give in to the subtle thoughts of not being good enough. The awful truth about outward beauty is that no matter how much time, attention, and investment you put into it, beauty can never really last. Our appearance inevitably changes over time, and our physical beauty does fade.

In a world where we are constantly told to beautify ourselves so we will be noticed, the concept of adorning the hidden person of the heart sounds almost make-believe. But what it comes down to is the truth that the most important opinion we should seek is the opinion of our Creator.

It might sound trite or cliché, but when we step away from the distraction of the media circus and all the lies it has told us, the truth becomes clear. Your gentle and quiet spirit is precious to God. You were made to delight the heart of God. Nothing delights him more than your heart, turned toward your Savior and clothed in the imperishable beauty of a peaceful spirit flowing with gentleness, kindness, and goodness.

> *How can you see gentleness and a quiet spirit affect your day-to-day life?*

Heavenly Father, as I hurriedly get dressed for the day, help me to remember that my inward beauty is more important than the outward. I don't always feel beautiful, even on the inside. I choose to dwell on the fact that you have made me beautiful. Help me to carry a gentle and quiet spirit into a busy world.

We also have joy with our troubles, because we know that these troubles produce patience, and patience produces character, and character produces hope.
ROMANS 5:3-4 NCV

A risk-free investment is too good to be true in the financial world. But spiritually speaking, there is such a thing. What is hard today, painful to give to God? Whatever that is, whatever you just can't release your grip on, go ahead and let go. You are not giving up for the sake of giving up, like throwing money into the wind—you are investing.

When you give your concern to God you can be fully confident that he will make a greater return than you ever could. He is beautifully abundant. In your struggles, he returns patience. When you feel like your patience is wearing thin, he returns character. When your character is being tried, he comes back with hope! Beautiful, joy filled, love inspired hope. And hope does not disappoint.

Don't be like a daughter who has a stick and refuses to trade it in for a prize her father is holding behind his back. Trust in the investment that God wants to make in you.

What concern are you ready to give to God today? Do you trust that he is a risk-free investment with great returns?

God, I trust you! You are good. I rest in the truth that you have good in store for me. You are the best risk-free investment that anyone can ever make. Thank you for your good returns on my small, limited investment.

Fortress

> *"Be my rock of refuge,*
> *to which I can always go;*
> *give the command to save me,*
> *for you are my rock and my fortress. For you have been*
> *my hope, Sovereign Lord,*
> *my confidence since my youth."*
> PSALM 71:3, 5 NIV

Did you ever build a fort as a child? Maybe it was made of blankets in your living room, with pillows stacked on top to keep the blankets from falling. Or perhaps it was a sheet draped over your bunk bed. Maybe you went to even greater measures and had someone help you build a tree house.

If you built a fort in the woods, it was most likely made of sticks, boards of wood, cardboard, and whatever else you happened to have around your house that could serve as walls or a roof. When you build, you make sure to have a few basics: a solid floor, walls, and something over your head to act as a protective shelter.

The fort we build today is our relationship with our God. He is our fortress: sturdy, unmoving, and strong. He is the solid ground beneath us, the sheltering walls around us, and the roof that protects us.

How do you put your hope and confidence in God's love? Can you believe that he is your strong fortress who will not be shaken and will never crumble.

God, thank you for your constant protection and sure footing beneath me. Thank you for your never-ending love and support.

Peace with Jesus

May undeserved favor and endless peace be yours
continually from our Father God and from our Lord
Jesus, the Anointed One!
2 CORINTHIANS 1:2 TPT

True peace can only come from Jesus. Peace that
gets deep inside your heart and settles there,
releasing any anxiety or fear you were carrying,
any worrying about what tomorrow might bring.
When you live for God, you understand that his
sovereignty makes worrying pointless. You are able
to rest, knowing your steps are determined and your
heart taken care of

It doesn't mean you get to do whatever you want,
but being in pursuit of a relationship with Jesus
does mean you experience freedom. Say goodbye
to baggage that has the potential to weigh you
down and restrict you from living the life you were
created to live.

When God formed you, you were made with a purpose. Only walking with Jesus allows you to live in that purpose. Pursue it whole-heartedly like you are on a mission. This is his hope for you!

> *How do you see God's purpose working in your life? Can you remain in his peace as you walk toward that purpose?*

God, thank you for being perfect peace for me. Thank you for creating me with a plan in mind, a roadmap for me to follow. I ask for your help in forging the way for me to live that life fully. I want to release all that I carry to you.

Never Useless

May our Lord Jesus Christ himself and God our Father, who loved us and by his grace gave us eternal comfort and a wonderful hope, comfort you and strengthen you in every good thing you do and say.
2 Thessalonians 2:16–17 NLT

Our words can have a big impact on others. What we say matters. How we live our life shows others who we live for. There are many situations we face where we can't find ourselves at a loss for words. We aren't sure exactly what to say. We know that nothing we do will help so we feel useless. What we can do is pray.

Ask for the Holy Spirit to intervene on your behalf and give you his words. He is eternally comforting, supernaturally hopeful, and he can bring strength when all human strength is diminished.

God wants us to speak goodness and mercy, and bring hope to the lost and broken. Often it is not within our reach to know how to do that, but God knows. Rest in that truth. Trust his words and know your goodness comes directly from him.

When do you find yourself most at a loss for words? In those moments, remember to pray for God's words to flow through you instead.

God, I'm not worthy to be delivering messages on your behalf, but people here need you. Help me to be a vessel for you however you see fit. Guide me in my conversations; give me the words I need and the strength from you to keep pursuing the lost in goodness and faith.

If we hope for what we do not see,
we wait for it with patience.
ROMANS 8:25 ESV

Hope springboards from faith. Faith expresses confidence in the unseen truths; it is a prerequisite to all spiritual understanding. How powerful it is! Hope takes this faith and looks forward to the future. Herein lies patience.

In times of need, your faith produces hope that drives you forward, patiently. You see your position more clearly through Christ's eyes, and you consider his faithfulness and its impact toward your potential.

You can confidently expect good in your future, because you know all things will pass except faith, hope, and love. Therefore, you can patiently work forward in God's plan for your life, fueled with resolve, doing what is in your hands to do.

Can you be patient and wait on God as he fulfills his promises and shows the glory of his goodness?

God, you have given me ample opportunity to hope! Your faith transforms my future, directing me even now. Please help me follow you, patiently, every day. Remind me of my blessings, so I will exalt you and keep you in mind all day.

*Many waters cannot quench love,
neither can floods drown it.
If one offered for love
all the wealth of one's house,
it would be utterly scorned.*
SONG OF SOLOMON 8:7 NRSV

We too often underestimate love. We think of it as something tame—a feeling we have the power to either conjure or suppress. But love is a force more powerful than floods and raging waters, more valuable than all the wealth we could offer.

If we understood the incredible power of love, we would understand how love itself compelled God to give up his deity for the sake of it. We begin to recognize how we—in our imperfection, our sin, and our rebellion—were worth giving everything for.

God is love, and nothing can buy, destroy, or even replicate that. All we can do, in light of the power of his love, is accept it: without trying to purchase it, without trying to find a way to negate it—simply just accept it.

> *The most powerful force in the universe is also the most gentle. How can you grasp hold of God's powerful love today?*

Thank you, God, for loving me enough to give up everything for me. Thank you for your love. Help me to rest and accept your love without trying to pay you for it or talk myself out of receiving it.

"Teach them to faithfully follow all that I have commanded you. And never forget that I am with you every day, even to the completion of this age."
MATTHEW 28:20 TPT

Life is made up of seasons and for many of us, different people are a part of each of those seasons. Yes, your family was more than likely there from the beginning, but then you married and started a new family in which your nuclear family was far less involved. You lived a whole life before your spouse, before your children. Rarely does someone have another person who was literally there through every moment of their life.

God is the one person who has known you in every season, more intimately than anyone else. He sees everything that makes up your heart, and he knows all the experiences that have come together to create your unique outlook and personality.

God is the only faithful one—the one that is there through every season of your life—and he will be with you forever.

> *How do you see God's faithfulness in all the seasons of your life? Are there times when he feels more near than others?*

Thank you, God, that you have been with me through everything. I know that you understand me fully because you know everything I have gone through—even the things I have told no one about. Thank you for your faithfulness to me.

Let him turn away from evil and do good;
let him seek peace and pursue it.
1 Peter 3:11 NKJV

There you are, sitting in traffic. Who plans to sit in traffic? Who wants to? Nobody. Or maybe your car is on the side of the road, one tire blown. Who has time to change a tire? Who wants to be haggling with insurance and the tow truck? Nobody!

The analogies of the road are simple situations that we have all found ourselves in, but the reality is a wide span of road bumps along our map of life can throw us into frustration and discord. Jesus asks us to trust. He is the one who knows the path of our lives and is at work in the world around us.

Often our route is too direct to build character and touch other lives. God wants to use you in this world. Set down your own agenda and look for his road map! When situations don't quite go your way, instead of turning to frustration, turn to peace. Trust that God knows the directions you need to take far more than you ever can.

What bumps and detours can you embrace today? Can you walk in confidence and peace knowing that God wants to use you in the world around you?

Thank you, God, that you are in control, and that I can have peace knowing that. Help me to peek through the clouds to find your glory in everyday moments and share it with others.

For seven days celebrate the festival to the Lord your God at the place the Lord will choose. For the Lord your God will bless you in all your harvest and in all the work of your hands, and your joy will be complete.
DEUTERONOMY 16:15 NIV

When you hear the words spiritual disciplines, do you think of prayer, fasting, or meditating on Scripture. If someone mentioned celebrating, would you rebuke them? Find their answer distasteful, unspiritual, irreverent?

Would you be surprised to find that God actually commanded us to celebrate, to rejoice, to have a party? When you see a beautiful sunset, you want to run and grab someone to share it with. When people graduate, get married, or have a baby, we celebrate! Are these things unholy? The exact opposite! It is right to celebrate the goodness of the Lord. To stir up joy and let it overflow into the world around us.

It's ok to laugh, to dance, to celebrate what God has done in our lives. He is good!

Gather around a campfire and sing your lungs out. Spin around the living room. Delight in a meal with friends. Make a list of other ways you can stir up joy in your heart.

Thank you, God, for the abundance of blessing in my life. I celebrate you and the wonder of who you are. I dance

*Work with enthusiasm, as thought you were working
for the Lord rather than for people.*
EPHESIANS 6:7 NLT

At times, our day-to-day work, whether that is a desk
job, or caring for little ones, or serving others in a
different capacity, can feel draining. God's gentle
reminder in Ephesians encourages us to focus on
the true audience in the work we are doing. Who
sees you? Is it just the people you are serving? No,
your audience is the Lord.

God knows the nature of your heart as you work.
He sees your selflessness and care, and he is the
only one who truly matters. It isn't always easy to
remember that when you are knee-deep in work
pressures, but remember he sees you.

God sees the work you put in and he appreciates you for it. Let this put a bounce in your step today.

Are you feeling drained today? What can help you push through these feelings and enjoy your day?

God, remind me today that you see me. As I work, may I feel joy in what I'm doing because I'm serving you first and foremost.

> *"His master said to him, 'Well done, good and faithful*
> *servant. You have been faithful over a little; I will set*
> *you over much. Enter into the joy of your master.'"*
> MATTHEW 25:21 ESV

Imagine hearing these words from God when you enter the pearly gates: "Well done, good and faithful servant, well done." Does it make your heart do a little pitter patter? Can you even imagine? Let's hope so. This is what we should be striving for.

We shouldn't be concentrating on how successful we are in our job, how fantastic our home looks for morning coffee, if we've climbed the corporate ladder, or satisfied every member of our congregation with our latest message. We should be focused on heavenly things, on our relationship with Jesus, on how well we are loving other people in his name. In all we do, are we serving and pleasing him?

He knows our hearts. He knows our humanness. He understands our weakness. He doesn't expect perfection. There is much grace in our relationship with him. But how thrilling would it be to hear those words and know we truly had given it our all.

What can you do today to test whether or not you are focused on heavenly things?

Jesus, above all else I want to be faithful to you. I want to be loving to those you ask me to love. I want my relationship with you to be at the forefront of my heart and mind. I want to be a good and faithful servant to you.

> *Behold, I will do a new thing,*
> *Now it shall spring forth;*
> *Shall you not know it?*
> *I will even make a road in the wilderness*
> *And rivers in the desert.*
> ISAIAH 43:19 NKJV

Our dreams, though they seem far off, were placed in our hearts for a purpose. And maybe they won't look exactly the way we always thought they would, but they'll still come true in a new way. Maybe the things that seem insurmountable to us will be easily overcome when we simply shift perspective and look at them differently.

We serve a God who is powerful enough to make a path appear right through an empty wilderness and create a stream of life-giving water in the midst of a desert. He is more than able to take even the most impossible of situations and provide clarity, direction, and the means to make it through.

Trust God with your impossibilities and rely on his strength for your weaknesses.

What seems impossible to you today? What have you given up on, walked away from, or written off as absurd? What dreams have you let die simply because you felt they were unattainable?

God, I bring my dreams before you and ask you to breathe life into the ones you desire for me. Make a way where there isn't a way. I trust you.

Start over with me,
and create a new, clean heart within me.
Fill me with pure thoughts and holy desires,
ready to please you.
May there never be even a shadow
of darkness between us!
May you never deprive me of your Sacred Spirit.
PSALM 51:10-11 TPT

Springtime is a great time to clear out the clutter and give your home a redo. It feels good to be able to sift through everything you've been hanging on to, and get rid of the things that aren't working for you anymore. That pile of things to be donated shows the progress you've made.

In the same way that our homes need to be cleared of all the useless items we collect over the years, our souls can use a good refreshing too. Over the years we collect bad habits, wrongful ways of thinking, and relics of our old lifestyles—ones that no longer fit our lives.

It's time to sift through your heart! Make a pile of the spiritual clutter. Stack it up, take one last look, and then be done with it. Progress is a beautiful thing!

What are you hanging onto that doesn't fit with how you want to live your life now? Why are you keeping it around?

**God, help me sift through my heart.
Help me decide what I need to clean out.
Show me how to get rid of the clutter
so I can walk in freedom and peace.**

> *Behold, the Lord's hand is not so short*
> *That it cannot save;*
> *Nor is His ear so dull*
> *That it cannot hear.*
> ISAIAH 59:1 NASB

Do you have regrets in your life that you wish you could take back? Things that you aren't proud of? You lay awake at night thinking about mistakes you've made and you wonder if you've gone too far to ever get back.

When Jesus hung on the cross, there were two thieves hanging beside him. One of those thieves, as he hung in his final moments of life, asked Jesus for grace and a second chance. That thief—minutes before death—was given forgiveness and eternal life. The very same day he entered paradise as a forgiven and clean man. In light of his story, how can we ever say that it's too late to turn it all around?

If you feel like it's too late to change something in your life for the better, remember the story of the thief on the cross. There is always hope in Jesus.

Do you feel like you need another chance? Like you've wandered too far to get back? Tell God about it and let him help you walk in newness of life today.

God, thank you that your love has no end and your grace knows no boundary. There are many things I'm not proud of in my life, but when I confess them to you, you throw them away and draw me close.

> "When you pray, do not be like the hypocrites, for they
> love to pray standing in the synagogues and on the
> street corners to be seen by others. Truly I tell you, they
> have received their reward in full. But when you pray,
> go into your room, close the door and pray to your
> Father, who is unseen. Then your Father, who sees what
> is done in secret, will reward you."
>
> MATTHEW 6:5-6 NIV

Cherish the secret things. So much of our life is for
others. So much. Whether it is the requirement of
jobs, keeping up relationships, or the programs we
volunteer for, a lot of our time and energy is spent
on other people.

God wants our time. He wants it for us and for him.
Maybe this will require a designated prayer closet,
or a quiet place away. Find it today.

Head to a quiet place with your Bible as soon as you get a chance. You might have to read this with noise all around you. What's important is that you dedicate your time to God. However you get your time, your heavenly Father sees you. What a faithful gift that thought is; he sees you in secret and will meet you where you are.

Can you get away today in secret to pray?
In secret, God will reward your heart.
Make sneaking away with him a daily routine.

God, I pray that I don't become religious with the way that I spend time with you. I want to engage with you at any moment of any day, and I don't need it to be loud and pretentious. Let me be genuine in my prayers to you. Thank you that you see me. Thank you that we don't have to make a fuss about this time, but it's something that we can both enjoy without trying to let everyone else in on it.

Truly Special

You are a chosen people, a royal priesthood, a holy nation, God's special possession, that you may declare the praises of him who called you out of darkness into his wonderful light. Once you were not a people, but now you are the people of God; once you had not received mercy, but now you have received mercy.
1 PETER 2:9-10 NIV

We all want to believe that we are special. Most of us grow up being told that we are, and it feels good to believe it. But over time, we look around us and realize that, really, we are just like everyone else. Doubt begins to creep in, making us second guess ourselves and damaging our self-confidence.

Long before you were even a wisp in your mother's womb, you were set aside and marked as special. You were chosen to be God's special possession, and that's pretty amazing. Revel in that knowledge this evening. He is calling you out of the darkness of the ordinary, and bringing you into the light of the extraordinary.

God picked you. He loves you. He wants you. Trust in that and let it change the way you think about yourself.

> *How did God shine his light into your heart?*
> *Be thankful that you now experience*
> *his mercy each day.*

God, help me to accept that I am special and chosen today. Give me confidence that I can make an influence in this world even today, because you have chosen me to be in this place for a purpose. Thank you for your mercy that can cover any wrongdoing in my day and start me afresh for tomorrow.

"Stop wailing," Jesus said. "She is not dead but asleep."
They laughed at him, knowing that she was dead. But
he took her by the hand and said, "My child, get up!"
Her spirit returned, and at once she stood up. Then
Jesus told them to give her something to eat."
LUKE 8:52-55 NIV

Do you know who you belong to? Your father and
mother rightly claim you as their child, but do you
recognize Jesus as the one who also calls you his?
He knows your coming and going, and your every
inner working. You are his.

How difficult it is to put our needs into the hands
of the Father. Do we dare hope? Imagine watching
a child die and feeling the despair of her absence,
as the father of the girl in the story of Luke must
have done. Then Jesus claims that she is only asleep!
Both the girl's father and Jesus love the child, and
both can claim her as their daughter, but only Jesus
commands her spirit and her life. His child hears his
voice and obeys his command.

When you truly recognize that you belong to God, trusting him with everything becomes your new normal. And what a great normal that is!

Where is God directing you today? Are you in need of healing or hope? Put your needs into his hands and watch what happens.

God, you are faithful to the deepest needs of my heart. You know me full well. Help me to hear your voice today let my spirit be renewed.

"If you keep quiet at a time like this, deliverance and relief for the Jews will arise from some other place, but you and your relatives will die. Who knows if perhaps you were made queen for just such a time as this?"
ESTHER 4:14 NLT

Because God designed us to long for heaven, we have an innate tendency to look ahead. But how do we find satisfaction in where God has us right now without always running ahead to the next thing? How do we live our lives to the fullest right where we are when we have a deep longing to be elsewhere?

When Esther found out the king's plans to destroy the Jews, she must have thought that God made a mistake in having her marry him. She probably wished that someone else had been chosen to be queen. But God chose her.

You may feel like a situation in your life is impossible. You may wish you were somewhere else, or that someone else had been given your set of circumstances. But God chose you for such a time as this.

What situations facing you right now cause you to want to run away and hide? Can you see God's hand in those situations? Can you trust in his perfect plan?

Thank you, God, that you make no mistakes. You chose for me to be right where I am to accomplish the work you have for me here. Give me the strength to walk in that calling.

*We are surrounded by a great cloud of people whose
lives tell us what faith means. So let us run the race
that is before us and never give up. We should remove
from our lives anything that would get in the way and
the sin that so easily holds us back. Let us look only to
Jesus, the One who began our faith and who makes it
perfect. He suffered death on the cross. But he accepted
the shame as if it were nothing because of the joy that
God put before him. And now he is sitting at the right
side of God's throne.*

HEBREWS 12:1-2 NCV

God provides us relief from any bondage we carry.
He truly does. Our Father can take any mistake
we've made in the past and release the beauty in
that error. We don't need to be so hard on ourselves.
We don't need to feel trapped, or think we've failed,
or hold on so tightly that we can't see the joy in our
current circumstance.

Have you been stressed about being trapped in sin
or burdened by worry? Turn your face toward God

and let him break your bondage apart. He can take the journey and form it into a place of humility and empathy for others.

Watch as the chains break and you walk away much, much lighter.

What are the mistakes you've made in the past that you have trouble letting go of? Take a few minutes to let God's promise of redemption make way into your heart. And then forgive yourself.

Jesus, thank you for your forgiveness. Thank you that you keep cheering me on even when I stumble. Be gracious to me today, so I can persevere in all that you have laid before me. Help me to have the end destination in mind. Please let me see beyond the wrong things I have done, as you do. Help me to know that you are creating a positive witness out of my walk with you.

Our people must learn to do good by meeting the urgent needs of others; then they will not be unproductive.
TITUS 3:14 NLT

Are you in a pattern of always saying yes? Afraid of letting others down? Sometimes saying yes feels really good…until it doesn't.

When we long to say no—when we crave a moment of peace or a commitment-free week—that list of yes items can seem like an unattainable mountain. Constantly saying yes leads to exhaustion and a less-than-our-best self. Carrying that feeling around is much worse than choosing to say no.

Are you being asked to do things that are beyond your capacity? Pray for the courage to say no when you need to. Making time for yourself is admirable; desiring more margin in your life for simplicity is okay—that is something to say yes to. Think about what you could refuse, and ask for God to help you be ok with saying no.

In what areas of your life do you crave more space?

God, there will be times today, when I need to say no. Give me the wisdom and discernment as I prioritize what is right for me to do, and right for me not to do. Give me grace as I respond to the requests of others. I need your help to prioritize. Guide my heart and my mind to have an understanding of what is good and what is not good for me to get involved in. Continue to give me wisdom.

> *He gives us more grace. That is why Scripture says:*
> *"God opposes the proud*
> *but shows favor to the humble."*
> JAMES 4:6 NIV

Some of the most substantial and ultimately wonderful changes in our lives come from moments of vulnerability: laying our cards on the table, so to speak, and letting someone else know how much they really mean to us. But vulnerability takes one key ingredient: humility. And humility is not an easy pill to swallow.

Isn't it sometimes easier for us to pretend that conflict never happened than to face the fact that we made a mistake and wronged another person? It's not always easy to humble ourselves and fight for the resolution in an argument—especially when it means admitting our failures.

Does your pride get in the way of vulnerability, or are you willing and ready to humble yourself for restoration in your relationships?

Who are you in the face of conflict? Do you avoid apologizing in an attempt to save face? What can you do today to humble yourself for the sake of a restored relationship?

God, you say that you will give favor and wisdom to the humble. Help me to show humility in my relationships. Help me to be authentic with the people I love and trust for the sake of building and restoring relationships.

Each of you should use whatever gift you have received to serve others, as faithful stewards of God's grace in its various forms.
PROVERBS 22:4 NIV

We all have something we feel most alive when doing. Call it a hobby, a talent, a passion—our niche. When we find that thing we both enjoy and excel in, it's one of the most special discoveries.

God has created us each with a unique skill set. He blessed us with talents that both distinguish us from others and complement us with others. He gave us these gifts so that we, as a whole body of believers, could further his purposes and advance his kingdom.

God gives us gifts so that we can be confident in them for his glory! Seek to be an active participant in the kingdom of God using the tools that he specifically chose for you.

> *Think for a moment about the specific gifts God has given you. Now think about your gifts in direct relation to the kingdom of God. How can you use your gifts to benefit the church, the community, and the world?*

God, thank you for making me special. Thank you for giving me different gifts and strengths than those around me. Help me to use those gifts to serve and bless others instead of just keeping them to myself.

Those who are dominated by the sinful nature think about sinful things, but those who are controlled by the Holy Spirit think about things that please the Spirit.
ROMANS 8:5 NLT

We think constantly about what we feed our bodies. Whether we eat healthy food or junk food, we are at least aware of what we are consuming. It's a simple principle: what you put in, you will get out. We know that if we continually feed ourselves junk food and candy, we will have low energy and poor health. We also know that if we eat balanced meals, we will feel better, look better, and function better.

Our thought patterns can easily be compared to our eating habits. When we fill our minds and hearts with things that aren't of God, our thoughts will follow those directions. Our thoughts determine our actions and our words.

When we meditate on Scripture and fill our minds with Godly things, our thoughts, words, and actions will naturally be those of life, peace, and truth.

What is governing your mind? Your flesh, or the Holy Spirit? Think carefully about what you put in, recognizing that it has a direct effect on what will come out.

God, help me to carefully control what I let my mind dwell on. I want my words and actions to reflect your goodness, love, and truth.

As God's chosen people, holy and dearly loved, clothe yourselves with compassion, kindness, humility, gentleness and patience.
COLOSSIANS 3:12 NIV

Fashion comes and goes. It can be really fun to see what's new in stores each season, finding pieces that update our look and wardrobe. There's nothing quite like the feeling of finding an item that makes us feel great every time we put it on—that one thing we knew was "it" when we saw it in the store.

Fashion is fun, but God calls us to clothe ourselves in something even better than the latest look off the runway. He wants us to get dressed in something that will make us feel even better than our favorite sweater or a great pair of heels. We are to be clothed in beautiful character traits that emulate Jesus Christ.

What are you wearing today? Are you all dressed up in compassion? Have you covered yourself with a dose of humility? Is gentleness draped around you, and patience your perfume? Trends in fashion may come and go, but these clothes never goes out of style. Wear them proudly today.

> *What attribute of the Spirit do you need to clothe yourself in right now?*

God, let me clothe myself with compassion, kindness, humility, gentleness, and patience today. Guide me to live in these gifts of the Spirit each day. Thank you that you don't care much about what I wear externally. As I read more from your Scriptures each day, I pray that you would teach me how to live by your Spirit so I can be clothed in your beauty.

Rest in the LORD and wait patiently for Him.
Those who wait for the LORD, they will inherit the land.
PSALM 37:7-9 NASB

Man can spend a lifetime studying God and never really understand the ways in which he moves: unexpected and unpredicted despite the prophecy of man, subtle yet monumental despite the theology of his character.

Abraham was told to look to the skies; his descendants would be as many as the stars. He was promised the future of mankind and a legacy that would shake history. Abraham was handed his dreams in one stunning moment by an almighty God. And then God was silent. All Abraham was left with was a barren, scoffing wife, a shocked expression, and an inky black sky filled with millions of stars representing impossible promise. But in his own timing, in his own way, God moved.

God has a timetable. You may feel like he has forgotten about you or that he's grown silent over the years. But God will honor the promises he's made to you. He will not forget to complete the work that he has begun.

> *What work are you waiting for the Lord to complete in you? How can you be patient while continuing to hope for his promises?*

God, you have a master plan, and you will accomplish it. Help me to be faithful even in the waiting and the quiet, knowing that at the right time, in the right way, you will move.

What a heavenly home God has set for the sun,
shining in the superdome of the sky!
See how he leaves his celestial chamber each morning,
radiant as a bridegroom ready for his wedding,
like a day-breaking champion eager to run his course.
He rises on one horizon,
completing his circuit on the other,
warming lives and lands with his heat.
PSALM 19:4-6 TPT

As we appreciate the beauty of the season, God has a fine eye for loveliness too. He is the ultimate painter, creating a beautiful canvas all over the world as it awakes. He wants each of us to be embraced in the warmth of the sun as we are reminded of his warmth and love.

Look up! Turn your face toward the sun. Let its warmth come over you. God is working in all things—even through the sunshine. Just as its light touches every corner of the earth, the Lord is working in every area of your life.

Allow him to do his work in you today. Take time to notice the ways in which he is touching you with his warm embrace. Let your heart be expectant about the possibilities of tomorrow. He is making your life into something beautiful. As you wake up with the sun, let your life embrace the light of his love.

Take time to notice the ways in which God is touching you with his warm embrace.

God, just as the sun's light touches every corner of the earth, you are working in every area of my life. I want to be a willing participant, letting you work on me today.

Here's the one thing I crave from God,
the one thing I seek above all else:
I want the privilege of living with him
every moment in his house,
finding the sweet loveliness of his face,
filled with awe, delighting in his glory and grace.
I want to live my life so close to him
that he takes pleasure in my every prayer.
PSALM 27:4 TPT

If there is one thing that we can appreciate, it's
something pretty. Shiny things easily catch our
attention, and we seek to surround ourselves with
beauty. There is much beauty to be found in our
natural world.

There is nothing wrong with finding loveliness in
our world, but if there is one thing that is more
beautiful than anything else, it is the Lord God
himself. His love, his mercy, his grace, and his
understanding—it is nothing short of breathtaking.

Don't miss the beauty of the Lord today. Seek it. It's there to be found!

You've been created to enjoy all that is exquisite, beautiful, and captivating. Give in to that desire, and find it in him!

God, thank you that everything around me that is beautiful gets its beauty from you. You are the most wonderful, glorious being in all of time and space. I want to spend time with you, breathing in your beauty and grace.

Have mercy on me, Lord, for I call to you all day long.
Bring joy to your servant, Lord, for I put my trust in you.
You, Lord, are forgiving and good,
abounding in love to all who call to you.
Hear my prayer, Lord; listen to my cry for mercy.
When I am in distress, I call to you,
because you answer me
PSALM 86:3-7 NIV

All too often we find ourselves, in our very full and busy lives, utterly alone. We feel misunderstood, an outcast of our doing. We isolate ourselves in a world of pain, feeling as though there is no one to whom we can turn.

There is good news! There is someone who always answers when we call. God is waiting for us to call on him. He has enough love to go around—enough for anybody willing to seek it out. We cry for mercy, and he hears our cries.

Whatever you are going through, call on him for support today. Scripture says he is forgiving and good. He wants to love you through your pain, and bring you out of your misery. He will answer you if you are willing to ask him for help.

What do you need from God today? He is listening.

God, sometimes I feel alone even in the busyness of my life. Help me to recognize that you are waiting to be with me. That you want to spend time with me and show me how much you love me. Thank you for your mercy and forgiveness. You are so good to me.

God's splendor is a tale that is told;
his testament is written in the stars.
Space itself speaks his story every day
through the marvels of the heavens.
His truth is on tour in a starry-vault of the sky,
showing his skill in creation's craftsmanship
PSALM 19:1-4 TPT

Have you ever felt the song of your heart praising the Lord? No words may come, no verses, no chorus, and yet your very being feels as though it may burst from the music inside you. You are not alone. Even the very heavens praise God in this way!

The Bible tells us that without words, and without even the slightest sound, the skies burst forth in a song of praise for the glory of God. Isn't that an amazing picture? Can't you just envision an orchestra above you?

Break forth into your song. Allow your heart to feel the words, even if you cannot fully form them. Give

God all your praises today. He is so deserving of them. Let your heart be a celebration of your love for Jesus Christ. Give in to the melody of worship inside you.

Picture all of creation worshiping God the way he deserves to be worshiped. Thank him for his goodness to you throughout your life.

What song is on your heart right now? Worship God with your song now.

Heavenly Father, the heavens declare your majesty. As I think about the sun, moon, and stars, may I recognize your voice in your creation, calling me, beckoning me to join in the beauty of the song that they sing. I worship you today. My heart is full of your splendor, and I want that to spill out onto my day.

He is able also to save forever those who draw near
to God through Him, since He always lives to make
intercession for them.
HEBREWS 7:25 NASB

Do you ever sit down to pray and find yourself struggling to find where to begin? You stumble over your words, your mind draws a blank. You want to be obedient by spending time with the Lord, but you don't even know where to start.

The good news is that God intervenes for us in the midst of every type of struggle, including our prayer life. He's got our back in times of pain and misery. Why wouldn't he be there for us when we want to converse with him? He will give us the words to say when we find ourselves lacking. In fact, he will even go beyond that and give you a form of communication that words can't express!

When you find yourself searching for the right way to express what you want to say to God, know that he will intercede if you allow him to.

Spend some time sitting quietly, and let God takes the reins for you today. He knows your heart!

God, some days I just don't have words. Help me to share my heart with you. Maybe there are times I just need to listen. Teach me to be sensitive to your leading.

Little Foxes

Catch for us the foxes,
the little foxes
that ruin the vineyards,
our vineyards that are in bloom.
SONG OF SOLOMON 2:15 NIV

Foxes are known for their cunning. They're sneaky little things, hunting their prey on the sly. They're known for their ability to camouflage themselves, hiding as they circle, and then suddenly pouncing on their intended target. And then, they use their teeth to sink in, shaking their catch until the life recedes from them.

Our enemy is a cunning one, and he uses our sin and temptations in the same sly way. They're camouflaged in the corners of our minds where we don't even notice until it's often too late. We see it when we're already caught, and our sin is shaking us to the point where we're ready to give up and give in.

God wants us to be like vineyards that are in bloom. He's ready to catch the foxes that are our would-be predators. Look for the ways that sin might be hiding in your heart, and give it over to the Lord so that he can prevent the unnecessary shaking in your life.

What little foxes do you see sneaking around your vineyard? Can you make a plan to allow the Lord to help you catch those foxes?

God, you are so good. Thank you that you care about me, and that you want to help me with temptation and struggles. Help me to carefully guard my vineyard and be aware of the little foxes that are trying to creep in.

> *His Spirit joins with our spirit to affirm that we are God's children. And since we are his children, we are his heirs. In fact, together with Christ we are heirs of God's glory. But if we are to share his glory, we must also share his suffering.*
> ROMANS 8:16-17 NLT

We are God's children. Scripture confirms this for us, so we know it to be true. As his children, we can rest in the knowledge that we are set to inherit all that is his. While that doesn't exempt us from going through rough patches, the good news is that Scripture also tells us that we get to share in his glory. And that is excellent news indeed.

Glory isn't just something nice like a sunny day or a delicious piece of chocolate. It's downright fabulous. Resplendent beauty and magnificence are just a couple of ways to describe it.

Imagine the most beautiful place you've ever been, or the most amazing moment you've ever experienced. It pales in comparison to the glory of God—and we get to share it! Rejoice in this as you reflect on your day. Though you may experience suffering along the way, sharing in his glory is the best prize you could ever receive.

What are the things that are worrying you most about this season in your life? Reflect on the bigger picture today and set your heart on the future glory.

Lord, give me a good outlook for my day ahead. Thank you for providing me with a different perspective. I know I can get caught up in the worries of the world, and while that is real, your glory is also a reality for me. At times, I approach my day with dread, fear, or anxiety, but I know that ultimately this life goes beyond death—you gave me the reality of eternity. Thank you for that!

When you lie down, you will not be afraid;
Yes, you will lie down and your sleep will be sweet.
Do not be afraid of sudden terror,
Nor of trouble from the wicked when it comes;
For the LORD will be your confidence,
And will keep your foot from being caught.
PROVERBS 3:24-26 NKJV

A pilot watches the flashing red light. A mother searches frantically for her child between the aisles. A driver glances in the rearview mirror at an oncoming truck. Certain fears have a gripping embrace, paralyzing to the body. The heart pounds, pupils dilate, palms sweat.

Other fears overwhelm the mind, causing anxious thoughts and sleepless nights. How will the bills get paid this month? Will the doctor have bad news? Family members need help, friends are overwhelmed with suffering, and we can't make it all okay.

When fearful thoughts flood our minds, God's words of wisdom and comfort can get washed away. If we can learn to fully trust him, he will calm our fears and still our quickened hearts. We can be fearless because our confidence is in God and his promises.

What fears are holding you captive today?
Let the flood of terror subside
and be assured that God is your refuge.

God, thank you that you lovingly attend
to my every need. I don't need to be afraid.
I submit my worry to you today and ask you
to bring me your peace.

*What is causing the quarrels and fights among you?
Don't they come from the evil desires at war within
you? You want what you don't have, so you scheme
and kill to get it. You are jealous of what others have,
but you can't get it, so you fight and wage war to take
it away from them.*
JAMES 4:1-2 NLT

Temper tantrums are as common for adults as they
are for children; they just look different in action.
Children haven't learned to curb the screaming and
stomping of frustration or anger, while adults have
more restrained behavior. But the heart is the same,
and the reactions stem from the same provocation.

James cuts right to the heart of sin. We want
what we want but we don't have it, so we throw a
tantrum. It's amazing how simple it is! Watch a child
and this truth will play out soon enough. Watch an
adult, and it may be more difficult to discern, but
unfortunately it is there in all of us.

Praise God for his amazing grace, which is extended to us for this very reason. Let us submit to God's forgiveness and draw near to him for his cleansing and purifying grace. It washes over us, and our tantrums are forgiven. When we humble ourselves, he promises to exalt us. What more could we want?

What responses do you see in yourself that remind you of a child throwing a tantrum? Let those responses go, and remember that God's forgiveness and grace is so much bigger.

Thank you, Jesus, for your mercy and grace. You have extended it to me time and time again, and you don't seem to want to hold back now. I want to dwell on that today and use it to help change my attitude.

> *"I am about to go the way of all the earth, and you know in your hearts and souls, all you, that not one thing has failed of all the good things that the Lord your God promised concerning you; all have come to pass for you, not one of them has failed."*
> JOSHUA 23:14 NRSV

Do you remember the first thing that you failed at? Maybe it was a test at school, a diet, a job interview, or even a relationship. Failure is difficult to admit, especially in a culture that values outward success and appearance. We often hear it said that success comes from many failures, but we only really hear that from successful people!

When Joshua was advanced in years, he reminded the Israelites of all that God had done for them. Though they had been unfaithful to God many times, God remained faithful, and they became a great nation that none could withstand.

God had a plan and a purpose for the nation of Israel, and through his power and mercy he ensured that these plans succeeded. In the same way, God has a purpose for your life, and while you may fail, he will not. Take the opportunity today to submit your heart to his will. Know that not one good thing that God has planned for you will fail.

In what ways have you experienced God's faithfulness in your life?

Thank you, God, for all that you have planned for me. I trust that your plans will not fail. I am humbled by your faithfulness to me. I am sorry that I am not always faithful to you. Help me to submit to your heart and will for my life.

We love because he first loved us.
1 JOHN 4:19 ESV

God's greatest commandments are to love him
and to love one another. Loving him may come
easy; after all, he is patient and loving himself. But
the second part of his command can be difficult
because it means loving intrusive neighbors at
the backyard barbecue, offensive cousins at family
dinners, rude cashiers at the grocery store check-
out, and insufferable guests who have stayed one
night too many.

Loving one another is only possible when we love
like God. When we love out of our humanity, sin
gets in the way. Obeying the command to love
begins with his love. When we realize how great
his love is for us—how undeserved, unending,
and unconditional—we are humbled because we
didn't earn it. But he gives it anyway, freely and
abundantly, and this spurs us on to love others.

We represent Jesus Christ to the world through love. If we know how high and wide and deep and long his love is for us, then we have no choice but to pour out that love on others.

Are there people in your life who you find it hard to love? How does understanding God's love help you with that?

Jesus, when I truly receive your love, the intrusive becomes welcome, the offensive becomes peaceful, rudeness gives way to grace, and the insufferable is overshadowed by the cross and all that you suffered there. Thank you.

Glorious

> *On the glorious splendor of your majesty,*
> *and on your wondrous works,*
> *I will meditate.*
> PSALM 145:5 NRSV

Leaves changing from green to orange to red. Gently falling snow. A rainbow-colored sunrise. A sprout of newness in the dirt. The smell of freshly cut grass. The rustling of leaves in the trees. The smell of a pine tree. Billowy, moving clouds. Sunshine kissing your cheeks. It is amazing that our Creator would make all this for us to enjoy. It's glorious, really.

Days often go by without us stopping to notice the wonder around us. We forget to slow down. We ignore this incredibly beautiful world that God made for us to explore and enjoy.

Can you make time today to slow down, take a walk outside, and soak in God's presence that's all around you: in the beauty of the sunrise, in the gentle wind blowing through the trees, in the fragrance of a flower in bloom. It is amazing what a walk with a friend, a run through the woods, or the feel of bare feet on grass can do for your soul. Try to make that happen before the day ends.

Can you take time to get outside and enjoy all that God has created?

Creator God, give me an opportunity today to see your glory in your creation. Help me to stop in amazement at the beauty you have put into your world. Help me to discipline myself to get outside and notice the world around me. Thank you that your hidden glory is revealed when I take the time to consider the beauty of nature.

Risk

> *The LORD is my strength and shield;*
> *my heart trusts in him,*
> *and he helps me.*
> PSALM 28:7 NIV

Most great things in life take some risk. We probably can each say that we've taken some pretty dumb chances in life, but we have also taken some incredible ones. Some of our risks end in disaster, but others in sheer beauty.

One thing all risk has in common is that it teaches something. We never walk away unchanged. And while stepping out and taking the risk itself is scary, we discover our own bravery in it. Trusting God requires our faith, which is a risk. But taking a risk is necessary to follow God wholeheartedly. Of course, it's easier to sit on the sidelines. To slide under the radar. To live safe. But letting fear hold us back from taking a risk keeps us from the breathtaking possibilities of life.

Sometimes you just have to jump. You have to forget about the fact that it might hurt. You have to set aside what your own understanding is telling you, and trust in what God is saying. The kind of risk required for faith in God is the kind with the greatest reward.

What risks is God asking you to take for him?

Teach me to take measured risks for you today, God. I know that you want me to live a life of adventure, and when you ask me to step out, I know that it is a risk worth taking. You are the lover of my soul. You wouldn't ask me to take a risk if you weren't right there beside me. Help me to trust you as my strength and my shield.

> *"God is not a man, that He should lie,*
> *Nor a son of man, that He should repent;*
> *Has He said, and will He not do it?*
> *Or has He spoken, and will He not make it good?"*
> NUMBERS 23:19 NASB

When Adam and Eve were caught in their sin, they were ashamed. Instead of repenting, they tried to protect themselves by placing the blame somewhere else. It was the woman's fault, wasn't it? Or was it the snake's fault? God punished all of them; the truth is that they were each responsible for their own decisions.

Lies have been around ever since the Garden of Eden. We don't respond much differently than Adam and Eve did when we try to hide our wrongdoing. We are quick to create excuses for ourselves; nobody likes to feel ashamed. Unfortunately, because we know that we stray from the truth at times, we are often uncertain of the truth in others. This is human nature. But it is not God's nature.

God is fully divine; he cannot lie. What God has spoken is truth, so we can trust that his promises will endure. Do you sometimes doubt God's presence, or help, or goodness in your life? Take time to read his Word today and believe that these are his words of truth, and that they will prevail.

What truths of God can you declare right now?

Father God, I don't want to doubt your promises anymore. Thank you that you speak words of truth into my heart. Help me to discern what is from you and what is not. I'm glad that you are the unyielding truth. I pray that I would always check myself against your nature and your Word. I want to reflect your truth in all that I say and do.

*Because of our faith, Christ has brought us into this
place of undeserved privilege where we now stand,
and we confidently and joyfully look forward to
sharing God's glory.*
ROMANS 5:2 NLT

You pull up to the drive-through, place an order for
the coffee that will help start your day, and hear the
cashier's words, "Your order was paid for by the car
in front of you." This unexpected generosity gives
birth to humbling gratitude, and the day is now
overcome with God's presence. A stranger may
have been the instrument of kind provision, but the
inspiration is unmistakable.

God is the author of generosity, providing us with all
we need. Look at all he gave to Adam and Eve, and
how little he asked for in return! They walked in his
presence daily, enjoying authentic relationship with
their Father. "Just don't eat the fruit from that tree or
you will die." Even when they ate it, God provided
atonement for them.

We, like Adam and Eve, have sinned and deserve death. But Christ is our substantial provision! Some things, like free coffee at the drive-through, are small provisions. Others are subtle or unseen altogether. But he is working his love out in generous portions for us.

> *When was the last time someone showed you generosity? How about the last time you showed generosity? What can you do today for someone else?*

God, as if eternity in your kingdom weren't enough, you bless me each and every day, whether I acknowledge it or not. Thank you for your unexpected and unlimited generosity!

To all who mourn… he will give: beauty for ashes;
joy instead of mourning; praise instead of heaviness.
For God has planted them like strong
and graceful oaks for his own glory.
ISAIAH 61:3 TLB

How many thoughts does the human brain conceive in an hour? In a day? In a lifetime? How many of those thoughts are about God: who he is and what he has done for his children? Imagine your own thoughts about life—grocery lists, dentist appointments, song lyrics, lost keys—and your thoughts about God—his majesty, holiness, comfort, creativity—weighed against each other on a scale. Likely, it would tip in favor of the many details of human existence.

These temporary details overshadow the one comfort and promise we can rely on: the gospel of Jesus' birth, death, resurrection, and ascension for our eternal salvation. Wipe every other thought away and we are left with this truth. For those burdened by their sin it is of great comfort! Jesus came to give us new life!

You are not a weak sapling, limited by inadequate light and meager nourishment. You are a strong and graceful oak, soaring and resilient for the glory of God.

Let your thoughts stretch above the canopy of everyday human details to bask in this joy: he has given you everything you need in Jesus.

God, thank you that you relieve my heavy burden, turn my ashes into beauty, and replace my mourning with joy. I am yours and I am so grateful for that truth today. You give me everything I need.

Come Away

> *My beloved speaks and says to me:*
> *"Arise, my love, my beautiful one,*
> *and come away,*
> *for behold, the winter is past;*
> *the rain is over and gone.*
> *The flowers appear on the earth,*
> *the time of singing*
> *has come."*
> SONG OF SOLOMON 2:10-12 ESV

Some say that romance is dead. It's not for God: the lover of our souls. He desires nothing more than time with his creation!

It can be a little uncomfortable to have his gaze so intently upon us though. We're nothing special, after all! Not beauty queens, academic scholars, or athletic prodigies of any kind. We might not be musical, or crafty, or organized. Our house might be a mess, and we could probably use a manicure.

Do you feel a bit squeamish under such an adoring gaze? There is good news for you! You are, in fact, his beautiful one! And he does, indeed, want to bring you out of the cold winter. He's finished the watering season and it is finally—finally!—time to rejoice in the season of renewal.

Why do you feel uncomfortable under the gaze of the one who loves you more than anyone else ever could? The time has come. Will you arise and come away with your beloved?

God, thank you that you call me regardless of how unworthy I think I am. I want to follow your lead. I want to get away with you. Thank you for waiting for me.

Finding Peace

*You will keep in perfect peace
all who trust in you,
all whose thoughts are fixed on you!*
ISAIAH 26:3 NLT

What does chaos look like in your world? Crazy work deadlines, over-scheduled activities, long to-do lists and short hours? All the above? How about peace? What does that look like?

Most of us immediately picture having gotten away, whether to the master bathroom tub or a sunny beach. It's quiet. Serene. The trouble with that image, lovely as it is, is that it's fleeting. We can't live in our bathtubs or in Fiji, so our best bet is to seek out peace right in the middle of our chaos. Guess what? We can have it. Jesus promises peace to all who put him first.

How appealing is it to imagine being unmoved by the stresses in your life? Is it easy or difficult for you to imagine claiming this promise for yourself? Ask Jesus to grant you true peace; fix your thoughts on him and watch the rest of the world fade away. When it tries to sneak back in, ask him again.

> *What are you burdened by right now? Fix your eyes on Jesus and allow him to bring peace into that situation.*

God, I fix my eyes on you because I know that is the only way that I will find peace in my crazy world today. Bring peace despite everything that will go on around me today. True peace is knowing that you care about me, and that you care about my eternal salvation. I can rest in the knowledge that my eternity is secure. Let that be enough for me.

My heart rejoices in the LORD!
The LORD has made me strong.
Now I have an answer for my enemies;
I rejoice because you rescued me.
No one is holy like the LORD!
There is no one besides you;
there is no Rock like our God.
1 SAMUEL 2:1-2 NLT

Consider for a moment the most joyous time of your walk with Christ. Imagine the delight of that season, the lightness and pleasure in your heart. Rest in the memory for a minute, and let the emotions come back to you. Is the joy returning? Do you feel it? Now, hear this truth: The way you felt about God at the highest, most joyful, amazing, glorious moment is how he feels about you all the time!

What a glorious blessing! Our joy is an overflow of his heart's joy toward us; it is just one of the many blessings God showers over us. When we realize how good he is, and that he has granted us everything we need for salvation through Jesus, we can rejoice!

The season of your greatest rejoicing can be now, when you consider the strength he provides, the suffering from which you have been rescued, and the rock that is our God. Lift your praises to him and let your song be never-ending.

What is worth rejoicing about today? Sing a song of joy to God, offering him thanksgiving for his many blessings.

Father, your blessings don't depend on me feeling joyous. I experience your joy when I recognize your gracious and loving blessings. I want to be more aware of your blessings in my life. Open my eyes, God.

> *The ransomed of the Lord shall return,*
> *and come to Zion with singing;*
> *everlasting joy shall be upon their heads;*
> *they shall obtain joy and gladness,*
> *and sorrow and sighing shall flee away.*
> ISAIAH 35:10 NRSV

The sin and sadness of life can make it seem like an endless night, where we are continually waiting for the dawn of Christ's return. In the darkest of nights, it doesn't always help to know that he will return someday, because this day is full of despair.

He gives comfort. Don't lose heart. He is coming for you! It can be hard, because he seems to be taking a long time, but he is preparing a place for you. You are not forgotten in this long night; your pain is familiar to him. Keep your eyes fixed on him! Soon you will hear his voice! He is also longing for that moment.

We live for the promise of his return. This promise overcomes our pain, our longing, our desperation, and our limits. All things become bearable and light under the assurance of seeing Jesus, embracing him, and gazing on his beauty!

How do you feel about Jesus' return? Don't be anxious and don't give up hope. He is coming!

God, I know that one day your church will be made into a pure and spotless bride. Help me today to just marvel at you. To glorify you, believe you, and love you. I wait in eager expectation for your return.

The Spice Rack

We know that in everything God works for the good of those who love him. They are the people he called, because that was his plan.
ROMANS 8:28 NCV

Anyone who does any amount of cooking has a spice rack—that one place where all seasonings are kept within easy reach of the stovetop. There are some spices that get used consistently: garlic, salt, and pepper. And there are other spices that may only be used once in a while: cardamom, tarragon, anise. While those lesser-used spices may collect dust in the back of our spice cupboards, we still rely on them to bring out just the right flavor in that one particular meal.

Life is a lot like a spice rack. We shelve our experiences like spices: some make so much sense—like salt and pepper—we pull from them often, clearly recognizing their usefulness. Other experiences are more subtle and undeclared; sometimes we go years never understanding why we had them. But then, in one moment, our life recipe will call for a little saffron. And all at once, it will make so much sense. That experience we had—the one we thought we must've had by mistake—will be the only one that matters for that moment.

You might look at a particular time and only see failure or waste. When you can't make sense of why it happened, remember that God will work it all for his good because you love him.

What are you struggling to make sense of? Ask God, the mastermind, to work it out for good.

God, thank you for giving me a variety of experiences, talents, and opportunities. Help me to see this variety as a wonderful gift from you. Let me put some of those talents and experiences to good use today.

Creation itself will be set free from its bondage to corruption and obtain the freedom of the glory of the children of God.
ROMANS 8:21 ESV

Some days begin with praises on our lips and a song to God in our hearts. Humility covers us like a velvet cloth, soothing and delicate and gentle. The truth of God plays on repeat: "God is good! God is good! I am free!" and the entire world's darkness cannot interrupt the chorus.

But other days begin by fumbling with the snooze button and forfeiting the chance to meet him in the quiet stillness. Pride, then, is a sneaky companion, pushing and bitter and ugly, and we wonder if we will ever delight with God again. We feel bound.

The ups and downs should be familiar by now, perhaps, but can we ever become accustomed to the holy living side-by-side with our flesh? One glorious day, flesh will give way to freedom, and there will be no side-by-side. Only the holy will remain. This leaves praise on our lips and a song in our hearts, the unending chorus of his goodness, the velvet covering as we sit before his heavenly throne.

Do you know how much God wants you to rest in his presence? He is waiting and faithful and tender.

Father, when I spend time with you, there is no need to hide. I can be exactly who I am. Thank you for the freedom in your presence.

The slap of a friend can be trusted to help you,
but the kisses of an enemy are nothing but lies.
PROVERBS 27:6 NCV

When your close friend confronts you about
something you need to change, it can be frustrating.
Even if you know it's right, it's never easy to be
told what your weaknesses are. After one of these
frustrating moments in a deep relationship, it can be
natural for you to feel more drawn to other people
with whom you have a surface-level friendship. You
enjoy the easy-going nature of these friendships
because they require far less work than the deeper
ones.

Surface-level friendships may seem easier to
maintain than facing the honesty that comes with a
deep friendship. But they are only more appealing
because we haven't gone deep enough to get to
the brokenness. If we dive deeper, we find people
who are just as imperfect as everyone else.

Value the deep relationships in your life. It's not easy to find someone who sees all your mess and sticks around anyway. Those who are willing to tell you the hard things in order to encourage you in your walk with God are far more valuable than the friends who simply tell you what you want to hear.

Who are the friends in your life that build you up? Who are the friends that bring you down? Graciously submit your friendships to God.

Heavenly Father, thank you so much for the close friends that I have in my life! I depend on those friends and I know that sometimes we might disagree, but at the heart of it is a deep love for one another. Give me discernment between the friendships that encourage me and the friendships that bring me down. Give me wisdom to hold on to the true friends and to graciously let go of the others. Help me to bless my true friends today.

Eternal Perspective

God has made everything beautiful for its own time.
He has planted eternity in the human heart, but even
so, people cannot see the whole scope of God's work
from beginning to end.
ECCLESIASTES 3:11 NLT

Much emphasis is placed on figuring life out. We so easily become caught up in the here-and-now that we lose sight of the fact that life on earth is really only a blink compared to what our life will be in eternity.

Our entire agendas will shift when we begin to live with eternal perspective. Once we understand that the only things that will last are those of spiritual worth, we suddenly realize that our priorities must be adjusted. Our eternal worth must supersede our earthly value. We can be among the world's most wealthy here but be headed for eternal destruction. Or we could be living paycheck to paycheck in this life and be governor of half a kingdom in the next.

You have the unique opportunity to determine how you will spend your forever life. Serve God well with your one short life on earth, so that you can live endlessly with him in glory.

> *How is what you are doing right now preparing you for eternity?*

I want to serve you well today, God. I get caught up in all the distractions of this life but I know that eternity sits in my heart. Help me to uncover your eternal workings in my life today. Reveal something of long lasting worth to me. Thank you that you have started to make me beautiful and you will continue to make me beautiful right into eternity. I don't know what you are doing from beginning to end, but I trust that you know all things.

Christ had no sin, but God made him become sin so that in Christ we could become right with God.
2 CORINTHIANS 5:21 NCV

Think of the most beautiful love story you've ever heard. Romeo & Juliet, perhaps? Or a story of someone whose love seemed to transcend all commonality? What is the most beautiful thing about their love? Is it the poetry, whispered in soft stanzas? Or is it the beauty, the gorgeous sight they make together? Or is it the sacrifice, the things they gave up for love.

Love isn't easy because it requires sacrifice. True love requires laying something down for the sake of the one you love. Jesus laid down everything for us: his life, his glory, his deity, and his rights. He was the only person who was capable to condemn an entire human race, and he chose to condemn himself. We don't have a star-crossed lover who died in vain for a love story that would end in tragedy. Our lover is victorious and strong.

Jesus knew that unless he laid down his life, he couldn't be with us. His love for us is so deep that he cannot face eternity without us. You will never hear a greater love story. Jesus longs for you with a fervor that led him to his death. Respond to him tonight by allowing your heart to be romanced in his presence.

> *Who are you able to share Christ's*
> *love with this week?*

Jesus, I love you. Sometimes I don't feel like I deserve your love, and sometimes I realize that I can't love you perfectly like you love me. But whatever my inadequacies are, I choose to believe that you hold the best kind of love for me. Let me bathe in your love today. I reflect on the amazing work that you did on the cross for all humanity. I know you love me personally, but you also love the entire world. Help me to be someone that communicates your love to the world around me.

"I am the Lord your God,
who brought you up out of the land of Egypt.
Open your mouth wide, and I will fill it.
But my people did not listen to my voice;
Israel would not submit to me.
So I gave them over to their stubborn hearts,
to follow their own counsels."
PSALM 81:10-12 ESV

Stubbornness is a tricky attribute. There is often no opening for conversation with a stubborn person. They have their own idea about how things should be done, and they aren't usually willing to listen to the advice of others.

We can all be stubborn in certain ways. Unfortunately, our stubbornness sometimes comes out toward God. We feel his Spirit gently advising us, but we rationalize it away in our heads instead of allowing it to guide our hearts. God can do more in a month with a life fully surrendered to him than he can do in years with a life that's holding back.

Do you hear the gentle voice of God today? Don't forget what he has done for you. God wants to fill your mouth and use your life, but you have to open it up to him. Don't hold back. Give God every part of you, and follow his counsel rather than your own. Surrender your stubborn heart to him completely.

Is there any area of your life in which you have a stubborn heart toward God?

God, I am sorry for holding back from the things that you have asked me to do. I am afraid, embarrassed, and just a bit stubborn, like the people of Israel. I don't want to let my stubborn heart get in the way, so help me to trust you and let go so you can do what you want with my life. I know that you have done great things for me, and that you want me to listen to your voice. I know that you have my best in mind. I choose to submit to you in this moment so I can follow your wise counsel and bring glory to your name.

A Worthy Friend

Let all that I am praise the LORD;
may I never forget the good things he does for me.
He forgives all my sins
and heals all my diseases.
He redeems me from death
and crowns me with love and tender mercies.
He fills my life with good things.
My youth is renewed like the eagle's!
PSALM 103:2-5 NLT

God created you for relationship with him just as he created Adam and Eve. He delights in your voice, your laughter, and your ideas. He longs to fellowship with you just as he did with his first son and daughter.

The friendship God offers to us is a gift of immeasurable worth. There is no one like him; indeed, there is none as worthy of our fellowship than God Almighty, our Maker and Redeemer.

Train your heart to run first to God with your pain, joy, frustration, and excitement. His friendship will never let you down!

When life gets difficult, do you run to God with your frustrations? When you're overwhelmed with sadness or grief, do you carry your pain to him? In the heat of anger or frustration, do you call on him for freedom?

Jesus, you are a friend that offers comfort, grace, and freedom. Thank you for your mercy and love. I appreciate your friendship. Help me to be a good friend to you, too.

*This forever-song I sing of the gentle love of God
overwhelming me!
Young and old alike will hear about
your faithful, steadfast love—never failing!
Here's my chorus: "Your mercy grows through the ages.
Your faithfulness is firm, rising up to the skies."*
PSALM 89:1-2 TPT

God in his great power and faithfulness never fails us, never gives up on us, and will never leave us alone, out on a limb, to fend for ourselves. His love for us remains—regardless of our circumstances or our weaknesses—strong and immovable.

God's devotion to his children exceeds that of all parents, whose love for their children seems unmatched, but is only human. Not only does God match our love, he surpasses it. He is without limits, and nothing can ever change God's devotion.

This truth is overwhelmingly satisfying; when such devotion has been proven, what else could attract our gaze? Where else could our eyes find such beauty and purity as they do upon the face of Jesus? In awe, we recognize that his gaze is fixed right back at us, seeing us as a lovely and worthy prize. We can neither deserve this gaze nor escape it. We are flawed, but he is unwavering in his love for us.

> *Do you know that the Father is wholly devoted to you? His great love for you is yours to enjoy forever. How does this make you feel?*

God, thank you for your devotion toward me. You see everything that goes on in my heart and my mind. You watch how I act and respond to others. And yet you love me. You still want to be with me. I am in awe of a God who can love so fully.

True Satisfaction

*O my dove, in the clefts of the rock,
in the crannies of the cliff,
let me see your face,
let me hear your voice,
for your voice is sweet,
and your face is lovely.*
SONG OF SOLOMON 2:14 ESV

Stress threatens to get the better of us, and sometimes we just want to hide. Remembering that secret bar of chocolate in the pantry, we may scurry off to do just that: bury ourselves away with the temporary but sweet comfort that helps the world slow down, if only for a moment.

The same instinct can arise with God. We get overwhelmed by his ministry or overdue for his forgiveness or out of touch with his Word and lose track of who he is. Instead of running toward him, we hide from him and look for other ways to meet our needs. We cannot hide from him, and in love he calls out to us.

You cannot outrun his love for you, nor should you try. Instead, leave the false safety of the clefts and crannies and pantries with hidden chocolate. Feel the pleasure of his friendship.

> *God wants to hear your voice and see your face because he finds them sweet and lovely. Is there anyone else who can satisfy you so perfectly?*

God, I thank you for your complete and astounding love for me. You come search me out when I am hiding and you call me lovely. Help me to run to you for satisfaction when I am feeling the stress of life.

For of His fullness we have all received,
and grace upon grace.
JOHN 1:16 NASB

You know those days, the perfect ones? Your hair looks great, you nail a work assignment (whether client presentation, completed order, or getting twins to nap at the same time), you say just the right thing and make someone's day, and then you come home to find dinner waiting for you. It's good upon good, blessing upon blessing.

Being a child of the Almighty gains us access to that blessed feeling every day, even when our circumstances are ordinary or even difficult.

God's love is so full, and his grace so boundless, that when his Spirit lives in us, even a flat tire can feel like a blessing. Our status as beloved children of the King guarantees it, we need only claim it.

Do you see God's grace poured out upon you today? Thank him for it.

God, thank you for those wonderful days when I see your grace upon grace. Help me to be thankful for those times and to rejoice even when I'm not having one of those days.

> *The LORD has rewarded me*
> *according to my righteousness,*
> *according to the cleanness of my hands in his sight.*
> PSALM 18:24 ESV

What do you think of when you hear the word purity? Perhaps a nun in her convent—someone who keeps herself completely untouched by the temptations of the world—an innocent child, or a great religious figure?

Often when we think about purity we think of a lack of obvious, outward sin. But both purity and impurity are birthed in the heart and developed in the mind long before they become expressed in action. Our purity is measured, not in what we do or what we have done, but in the hidden places of our heart's attitudes and our mind's wanderings.

If you ever wonder if your purity counts for anything—if refraining from the pleasures of sin is even worth it—be encouraged today. God will reward you according to your righteousness. He sees the intentions of your heart and the thoughts in your mind. He knows how badly you want to please him with your life, and he will bless you for it.

How do you think purity matters? Is it worth refraining from the pleasures of the world? Trust in God's promise to reward the righteous.

God, thank you that you are honored in my purity. That is the most important reward of all. I want to glorify you with my life.

> *Moses said to the Lord, "Please, Lord, I have never been a skilled speaker. Even now, after talking to you, I cannot speak well. I speak slowly and can't find the best words."*
> EXODUS 4:10 NCV

When God asks us to do something, our first instinct is often to look around at who we feel could do it better. We wonder why God didn't choose that person, who—in our eyes—is clearly more qualified than we are.

God could have chosen anyone to be his mouthpiece and his leader for the incredible work he did with the Israelites. He picked Moses. He knew what Moses' strengths and weaknesses were before he called him. And he still picked Moses.

Do you ever feel like God shouldn't have picked you for something? Do you think it would have been smarter for him to pick someone who is more creative, more intelligent, or more eloquent? You may not understand why God picked you for a certain task, but you can trust that when he calls you to do something, it's because he knows that you are not only capable, you are the one he wants to do the job.

> *What are you doing right now*
> *that you see God has called you to?*
> *What is he calling you further into?*

God, I don't want to question you when you call me. I don't often feel qualified enough to do what you want me to do, and yet I can't ignore the call that you have on my life. Affirm that call to me now so that I can do whatever it is you ask of me. I look ahead to the calling that you have entrusted to me. You didn't give this to anyone else, you gave it to me. Give me confidence to continue in the good works that you have given me to do.

"Thus says the Lord who made the earth, the Lord who formed it to establish it—the Lord is his name: 'Call to me and I will answer you, and will tell you great and hidden things that you have not known.'"

JEREMIAH 33:2-3 ESV

"If you're there God, give me a sign!" People have screamed this into the heavens many times throughout the years. We want to see something that will tell us that God is real—and not just real, but also present. We want that experience that will bring heaven to earth and expel our doubt with a single lightning bolt.

God is more than able to give us those miraculous signs as we have seen countless times throughout the Bible and throughout history. But he is so much more than experience. We mistakenly think experience is the peak of his power. Other gods can perform miracles and deliver experiences, but the one true God continues to show his power in the valley. He is even in the valley of the shadow of death where miracles seem non-existent. Those other gods have nothing to offer us in despair.

God is present with you today and will show himself to you in different ways tomorrow. He shows us things we aren't even expecting. He is not limited by time, space, or human understanding. Put your hope and faith in the God who knows everything.

> *How has God shown himself to you*
> *in the small things recently?*

God, thank you for showing your power at times, but help me not so seek those out to validate who you are. Let my faith be enough to be assured of your presence and goodness in my life and your continued work in this world.

I lie down and sleep;
I wake again, for the LORD sustains me.
PSALM 3:5 NRSV

There is always something to worry about, isn't there? Whether it's health, finances, relationships, or details, there are many unknowns in life that can easily keep us worrying. But what if we stopped worrying? What if we stopped questioning and decided instead to feel peace? What if we could trust completely that God would take care of us and our loved ones. God is our rock and he alone will sustain us.

There will be many unknowns in your life. There will be moments when the rug feels as though it's been pulled out from under you, and there is nothing to do but despair. In those moments that you can't control, you can trust. You can rest your soul, your mind, and your body in the hands of the one who has the power to sustain you.

The words in Psalm 3 can bring us comfort and peace when we are fearful. It speaks volumes about the grace of God: the protection and safety of his hand. But the verse goes beyond peace and comfort to the power of God. We only wake up because of his sustaining power. When we trust and believe in this God who possesses the power of life and death, what do we have to fear? Our entire lives are in his hands. We can't change that fact, so we might as well rest in it.

What is interfering with your ability to rest? Ask God to give you a solution so you can rest physically and spiritually.

God, today I face the unknown. Let me rest in the knowledge that you will sustain me. I need that rest. I need to rest my body, and I need to rest my soul. I believe you have the power of life and death, so I ask that you will continue to sustain me.

Give freely and become more wealthy;
be stingy and lose everything.
The generous will prosper;
those who refresh others will themselves be refreshed.
PROVERBS 11:24-25 NLT

There is need everywhere we look. Families who
need homes, missionaries who need support,
food shelves that need donations, and non-profit
organizations that need finances. But how can we
even begin to meet those needs? How could we
possibly give enough to make a difference?

Generosity can be scary. Giving might mean that we
will have to do without. Giving costs us something.
We think that we have to have less in order to
do more. But in God's economy, he who gives
generously will be repaid lavishly. He who holds
nothing back will inherit everything.

Are you able to give to someone today? Remember that God will provide for your every need, no matter how much you give to others. He doesn't measure wealth the way we do. He doesn't operate on our economic system. He gives with rewards that will last forever, and wealth that will never run out.

> *What or who is God asking you to be generous toward?*

God, give me an opportunity to be generous. It feels a little scary for me to say that, but I know that you want me to be a generous giver, and I know that it will be good for me to give, and good for someone to receive. Thank you that each new day brings another opportunity to serve you and to serve others.

"The one on whom seed was sown on the good soil, this is the man who hears the word and understands it; who indeed bears fruit and brings forth, some a hundredfold, some sixty, and some thirty."
MATTHEW 13:23 NASB

Calla lilies are beautiful flowers with wide, spotted leaves, thick stems, and bold colors. Year after year, you can watch the stunning leaves appear, and anticipate the gorgeous flowers…and then be disappointed when nothing more happens. Perhaps the soil is the problem? Calla lilies can be very particular.

It's a great picture of Jesus' parable of the sower and the seeds. Some seeds fall on rocky soil, and while God's Word is received, it doesn't take firm root and quickly withers at the sign of hardship. The seeds that are established in good soil, where the roots can go deep, not only survive, they also bear fruit.

Be encouraged to hear the words of Jesus, and then allow those words to penetrate your heart deeply until you understand them. Plant yourself in fertile soil, and watch the beauty that emerges.

> *Do you hope to see more depth in your relationship with Jesus? Do you want others to see God's beauty displayed through your life?*

Father, I want to bear good fruit. I know that means I need to have roots that go down into good fertile soil. Help me to create that kind of environment in my heart.

When times are good, be happy;
but when times are bad, consider this:
God has made the one as well as the other.
Therefore, no one can discover
anything about their future.
ECCLESIASTES 7:14 NIV

It's easy to feel happy on a sunny day, when all is well, the birds are singing, and life is going along swimmingly. But what happens when waters are rougher, bad news comes, or the days feel just plain hard?

God wants us to feel gladness when times are good. He has made each and every day. We are called to rejoice in all of them whether good or bad. Happiness is determined by our circumstances, but true joy comes when we can find the silver linings, hidden in our darkest hours—when we can sing his praises no matter what.

We don't know what the future holds for us here on earth, but we can find our delight in the knowledge that our eternity is set in beauty.

> *Is your happiness determined by your circumstance? Pray that you will discover true joy in our Creator.*

God, give me a deep and abiding satisfaction in each day that goes beyond my human understanding. Help me to see the beauty in the future you have for me.

Do not conform to the pattern of this world, but be transformed by the renewing of your mind. Then you will be able to test and approve what God's will is—his good, pleasing and perfect will.
ROMANS 12:2 NIV

Wake up. Make bed. Get dressed. Coffee. Not always in that order, but you can guarantee that many do those things every single morning. They might also bite their nails, anger easily, and stay up too late. Patterns are hard to break. We are, after all, creatures of habit, and unfortunately not all of those habits are good.

What do you do when you are confronted with a habit that is not positive? Do you recognize when you rely on something just because it makes you feel accepted, comforted, or in control? Sometimes we aren't even conscious of our habits until we try to give them up.

The Scripture says that establishing the right pattern begins with the renewing of our minds. This means that we must first acknowledge the need for change, and then submit our way of thinking to resemble that of Christ.

What habits are you trying to break?
Can you trust God today to show you his good,
pleasing, and perfect will as you submit your
worldly habits to him?

Father, I need a renewed mind. I don't want to keep acting out the habits that are not good in my life. Help me to begin to train my mind with your Word. Show me your will so I can form good habits around that instead.

Whatever is true, whatever is honorable, whatever is right, whatever is pure, whatever is lovely, whatever is of good repute, if there is any excellence and if anything worthy of praise, dwell on these things.
PHILIPPIANS 4:8 NASB

Do you ever catch yourself dwelling on the negative aspects of life? We can be nonchalant when someone tells us good news, but talk for hours about conflict, worries, and disappointment. It is good to communicate things that aren't going so well in our lives, but we can also fall into the trap of setting our minds on the wrong things.

Paul saw the need to address this within the church of Philippi. It seems there were people in the church that thought too highly of themselves and allowed discord to reside in their midst. Think of what dwelling on the negative actually does: it creates feelings of hopelessness, discouragement, and a lack of trust in our God who is good, true, and just.

Find something in your life and the lives of others that has virtue and is worthy of praise.

Do you need to ask for forgiveness for a heart that has been too negative? How can you change the way you view things?

God, I choose to dwell on the true, noble, just, pure, and lovely things, and experience the refreshing nature of a positive outlook today.

> *Trust in the LORD with all your heart,*
> *And lean not on your own understanding;*
> *In all your ways acknowledge Him,*
> *And He shall direct your paths.*
> PROVERBS 3:5-6 NKJV

Trust can be a hard word to put into action mostly because our experience with others tells us that we can be sorely disappointed. People let us down in many ways. We can even be disappointed in ourselves.

Remember the trust game that involved standing with eyes closed and falling back into the hands of a few peers in hopes that they would catch you? There was risk involved in that game, and it didn't always turn out well. Nothing can truly be guaranteed in this life, can it? Well, it depends on where you place your trust.

God watches over us, cares for us, and is involved in our lives. When we acknowledge that every good thing comes from him, our faith is strengthened and we are able to trust him more.

Make a point of noticing how God directs your paths today, and thank him for being trustworthy.

God, I want to remain confident in you. I know you will accomplish what you have promised. When following you gets hard, help me to press in even harder and remember that you will direct my path.

> *Since the creation of the world God's invisible*
> *qualities—his eternal power and divine nature—have*
> *been clearly seen, being understood from what has*
> *been made, so that people are without excuse.*
> ROMANS 1:20 NIV

It doesn't take much to marvel at creation. Looking up into the night sky, sitting on a shoreline, hiking through a forest, or watching a bud begin to blossom, our encounters with nature are many. But we don't often take the time to truly notice how incredible creation is.

God chose to reveal himself to us in a profound way. He knew that we would have appreciation for the beauty of nature that surrounds us.

God's invisible qualities are represented through something visible. And we describe it as beautiful, awesome, and perfect. This is God.

Take a look around at God's creation today and dwell on the quality of God that is represented.

God, thank you for sharing your divinity and eternal power through your creation in a very real way. You are more amazing than anything I can fathom.

"If you wish to be complete, go and sell your possessions and give to the poor, and you will have treasure in heaven; and come, follow Me." But when the young man heard this statement, he went away grieving; for he was one who owned much property.
MATTHEW 19:21-22 NASB

If only I had more money! The thought runs through our minds frequently, and though we may actually have enough to be content with, we are often thinking about what we could do with more.

Wherever you stand financially, you probably have a goal of accumulating more wealth than you have now. But did you ever notice how the Bible seems to view earthly riches as actually getting in the way of our relationships with God and others?

Wealth is rarely what we hope it is; the more we have, the more we have to lose. Jesus wanted the rich man to have a compassionate heart—one that was willing to give up what he had for the sake of the kingdom. To do this, he would have needed to give up the life that he was accustomed to. Before asking God to bless you with wealth, ask him to bless you with a heart of giving.

Do you find yourself constantly on the lookout for more ways to make money? Do your finances consume a lot of your thoughts? Why do you think this is?

God, I want to have a heart of giving. Help me to think of others before I think of myself. I want to help those who have less than I do. Show me how.

Stars

Lift up your eyes on high
And see who has created these stars,
The One who leads forth their host by number,
He calls them all by name;
Because of the greatness of His might
and the strength of His power,
Not one of them is missing.
ISAIAH 40:26 NASB

If you have ever had the chance to be in a remote location on a clear night, you will know what it is like to look up into the sky and marvel at the magnificent display of stars. It is such a breathtaking view—one that reminds us of the greatness of our God.

Many times in the Bible, humanity is compared to the stars. We are reminded of how many people God has created. Yet, God says that he both leads and calls them by name. If the stars appear magnificent, then how much more magnificent is the one who created them?

We worship a God that is able to remember each of us by name, and to know that not one of us is missing.

Do you feel insignificant in God's great world today? Remember that God has a perfect plan for this world, and you complete this plan.

God, I lift up my eyes to you, knowing that you know my name. I am not missing from your plan. Thank you for giving me purpose.

Be Content

The LORD is all I need.
He takes care of me.
My share in life has been pleasant;
my part has been beautiful.
PSALM 16:5-6 NCV

She has great hair, looks energetic and fit, and has a doting husband and cute kids. She sings beautifully in church, is a great cook, and never says a bad word about anyone. She is smart and organized and holds a weekly Bible study at her house. She is everything we are not!

We spend a lot of our time comparing ourselves with others, and it can often lead to envy. God asks us to conduct ourselves in a way that is not envious, but content. When we compare ourselves to others, we choose to dwell on what we do not have rather than the good things that God has given us.

God created us as we are, and he declared his creation to be good. Furthermore, he has given us the gift of always being near. To know that Jesus is right next to us, all the time, is really all we need.

Are you able to realize God's presence with you today, and let that fill you with contentment?

Thank you, God, that you are always near me. You take care of me. You don't compare me to others. You see me just as I am and you love me. Thank you for this beautiful life that you have blessed me with. I choose to be content today.

Receive my instruction, and not silver,
And knowledge rather than choice gold;
For wisdom is better than rubies,
And all the things one may desire
cannot be compared with her.
PROVERBS 8:10-11 NKJV

If you were granted the one thing that you desire most, what would it be? We can probably answer this question better if we think of who or what we idolize. Whose life do we want, or what quality do we most admire? Beauty, intelligence, creativity, recognition, or love?

King Solomon understood the value of wisdom better than any other. When God offered him anything he desired, King Solomon responded with a request for wisdom. He could have asked for fame, or riches, or success in warfare; instead, he asked for understanding. King Solomon sought knowledge and instruction first, and ended up being the most wise, wealthy, famous, successful king that ever lived.

Silver, gold, and rubies are rare and precious elements. They are beautiful, strong, and valuable. But wisdom is so much better.

> *Do you own jewelry with precious metal and stone? Remind yourself of the greater value of wisdom today.*

God, I seek to understand your ways, your thoughts, your Word, and your people more than rubies and other precious stones. Wisdom holds so much more eternal value than riches, and I thank you for giving it to me freely.

The Word gave life to everything that was created,
and his life brought light to everyone.
The light shines in the darkness,
and the darkness can never extinguish it.
JOHN 1:4-5 NLT

Have you ever walked somewhere in the pitch black? You bump into things, knock stuff over, and often can't even place where you are or where you're going. Everything becomes muddled in the darkness. Without light to guide us, we can't see where we're going, or what we're running into.

Many times throughout the Bible, God likens being in sin to being in darkness. When we immerse ourselves in sin, thus rejecting the light of the truth, we can no longer see what we are running into. Darkness of sin will cloud our thinking and our rationale, and we won't even be able to determine what other sins are coming our way when we leave our sin unchecked. By allowing sinful messages to enter our souls through different avenues, we lose our ability to navigate our lives.

When wickedness begins to overtake your life, you lose the ability to recognize what is making you sin. Strive to keep your soul sensitive to the truth. Keep sight of the light by spending time in God's Word.

Who can you share the light of Christ with this week?

God, shine your light into my heart. Illuminate my sin so that I can repent and be free of the darkness. I want to walk without stumbling today. Thank you that darkness cannot stand up to light. Now that I know the truth of your ways, the darkness has been expelled and my faith in you will never be extinguished. Help me to shine the light into other people around me so they will be exposed to your truth.

Victory

*Thank God! He gives us victory over sin and death
through our Lord Jesus Christ.
So, my dear brothers and sisters,
be strong and immovable.*
1 CORINTHIANS 15:57-58 NLT

Have you ever watched one of those movie
battle scenes where the good guys are grossly
outnumbered? You wince as the evil army swoops
in with thousands of troops carrying sophisticated
weapons. While the good army has a lot of heart,
you know they don't stand much of a chance. But
when it all seems lost, there is that moment when,
out of nowhere, reinforcements arrive in a surge
of hope to assist the good army. Suddenly, they go
from losing terribly to winning victoriously!

Daily, we are engaged in our own battle against sin.
Left to ourselves, we don't have the strength necessary
to win the fight. But when it seems all hope is lost, our
reinforcement—Jesus Christ—arrives, and we gain the
strength to boldly obtain the victory over sin.

You may go through seasons in your life when you feel like sin has you outnumbered. Temptation is great, and you don't feel that you have the strength to overcome it. But know that you don't have to fight alone. You have the power of God on your side, and he has already won against sin and death. Embrace victory over sin as you thank Jesus for his work on the cross.

> *Where do you need to see the victorious Christ reign in your life again?*

Jesus, forgive my sins and help me to gain the victory over any darkness that would try and creep back into my life. I feel like I am confessing sin to you time and time again, yet I know you want me to recognize that I already have the victory. You won this victory on the cross and I no longer have to live in guilt and shame because you have set me free!

My little children, I am writing these things to you so that you may not sin. But if anyone does sin, we have an advocate with the Father, Jesus Christ the righteous.
1 John 2:1 esv

It says in Isaiah that no matter which way we go, we will hear a voice saying, "This is the way, walk in it." But it is often so hard to hear that voice—and harder still to distinguish it from the other voices in our lives.

You have a mediator between yourself and the almighty God. It is someone who loved you enough to lay down everything for you. Surely a man who loves you with that kind of intensity also loves you enough to forgive your imperfections?

We stumble and fall every single day. We hear wrong, and we miss the mark continuously. We fall into sin when all we were chasing after was righteousness, and we feel guilt even when we know we've been given grace. Rest in the fact that God is gracious, that he knows your humanity and he compensates for it.

How do you need to experience God's help in your life right now?

Thank you, Jesus, for helping me to overcome my sin. Thank you for showing me that there is a way out of sin, and that there is a better way. I am forgiven. Thank you for making me whole again, and for cleansing me from thoughts and actions that are not compatible with your kingdom.

> *"I am the true vine, and my Father is the gardener. He cuts off every branch in me that bears no fruit, while every branch that does bear fruit he prunes so that it will be even more fruitful."*
> JOHN 15:1-2 NIV

Take a moment to reflect on a time when you felt you were giving the best of yourself. You may be thinking of times when you were utilizing your gifts and talents and could witness your positive influence in others around you. You may not have to reflect back that far, or you could be wondering where those times have gone!

Jesus describes himself as the vine. If we are being nourished from that source, we will produce fruit. In the times where we feel like we are not flourishing, it may be that the Father needs to do some necessary pruning—for the health of both the branch and the whole vine.

Rather than despair over his pruning, be encouraged that God has seen the fruit you have produced and is allowing a period of dormancy so that you will flourish once again.

Take some time today to reflect on your gifts, submit them to Jesus, and wait expectantly for the great gardener to bring them back to life.

Father, being pruned doesn't always feel great, but I trust you. I know you have a reason for everything you do. Help me to receive your pruning, to learn and grow, and to produce more fruit because of it.

Do not participate in the unfruitful deeds of darkness,
but instead even expose them; But all things become
visible when they are exposed by the light,
for everything that becomes visible is light.
For this reason it says,
"Awake, sleeper,
And arise from the dead,
And Christ will shine on you."
ROMANS 8:15 NASB

Most people seem to agree that fitting room mirrors
are unpleasant. Something about that fluorescent
lighting draws attention to all of our flaws. We
would much rather admire our reflections in the
flattering light of a glowing campfire or a few well-
placed lamps. Bright light exposes every flaw. What
was concealed in the darkness becomes glaringly
obvious in the light.

God is very clear throughout Scripture that our sin
makes us dead. When we are entrenched in sin, it
is as though we are asleep. But when we bring our

sin out from the darkness and into the light, Christ shines on us and frees us from our bondage of sin and death.

The longer we hide our sin in low lighting and flatter ourselves in it, the longer we sleep and miss out on the good things that God has for us.

Release whatever secret, hidden sin you are clinging to today and bask in God's glorious light.

God, I don't want to hide in the darkness where I miss your goodness and blessing. Help me to come into the light. Thank you for your forgiveness and grace.

> *Know therefore that the LORD your God is God, the*
> *faithful God who keeps covenant and steadfast*
> *love with those who love him and keep his*
> *commandments, to a thousand generations.*
> DEUTERONOMY 7:9 ESV

How do you trust God when you feel betrayed by him? What strength is there for the moments when you feel as though the Creator of the universe has simply looked the other way? You know in your heart that he has control over every infinitesimal life, and yet he seems to have failed with yours. He promises peace, but your world is in turmoil. He offers joy, but pain is all you can feel. Dreams and purpose flooded your heart, and then were ripped from you.

Is God really faithful? Can he be trusted with our lives? With our hearts? Yes! He will keep his covenant to a thousand generations. That's roughly estimated as 20,000 years—a long time to remain faithful to someone. The same God that spoke to

Moses and led the Israelites out of captivity in a whirlwind of miraculous power is covenanted to do the same for us.

The God who called Lazarus out of his grave, is with you in the same measure of power. The God who loved David through all his sin and brokenness loves you just as steadfastly. Rest in his covenant and trust that he will keep his Word.

Do you have trouble trusting God?
Why do you think that is?

God, thank you that you are faithful. There is no doubt that you have been faithful to keep your promises and you will continue to do so. Help me to believe that in my heart.

Let everyone be sure that he is doing his very best, for then he will have the personal satisfaction of work well done and won't need to compare himself with someone else.
GALATIANS 6:4 TLB

In the age of social media, comparison has become an easier default for us than it's ever been before. When every image we see of others has been properly angled, edited, filtered, and cropped we are quickly led into the delusion that the lives we see portrayed in those images are perfect. We believe that the smiling faces we see in that post are always smiling, and the perfect homes with the beautiful lighting are permanently well-kept and polished.

The danger of these filtered images is that we end up comparing ourselves to something that isn't an accurate standard. What we don't see is the life outside that frame. We don't see the mess, the struggles, and the imperfections that are inevitably part of every life—even the perfect-looking ones.

God wants you to be so invested in the work that he has given you to do that you are not distracted or dissatisfied by what you see someone else doing. By diving headfirst into your unique life, you are saying yes to contentment and joy and moving forward into greater fulfillment and happiness.

How can you be sure that you are doing your very best? Do you compare yourself to others?

Father, thank you that you see me as unique. You don't want me to be like anyone else. Help me to be content in who you have created me to be. I want to do the things that you have given only me to do.

Whatever you do, whether in word or deed, do it all in the name of the Lord Jesus, giving thanks to God the Father through him.
COLOSSIANS 3:17 NIV

Have you ever noticed on vacation that your heart feels lighter? That you worry less and are more thankful? Cultivating a heart of thankfulness can shift our entire perspective on life. When we are grateful, we start to see the light of God more. We start to see him everywhere.

A thankful heart is a heart that refuses to let the enemy in and deceive us. Suddenly, our circumstances seem not so terrible, our problems not so huge. A heart of gratitude glorifies God and keeps us centered on him.

Allow Christ into your heart today, even though it will be full of things to do, people to see, jobs to take care of. Be thankful as you do the day-to-day things and cultivate that heart for giving thanks! A heart of thankfulness keeps you grounded in Christ and allows you to live the fullest life he's designed for you.

> *What can you do to start cultivating a heart of gratitude?*

God, be so present in my life today that I can't help but think about you and all the wonderful people and things you have placed in my life. Help me to be thankful even in times of trial. Thank you for the ups that make me smile and the downs that build resilience. Thank you for the good and the bad. Help me to be thankful in everything.

Since, then, you have been raised with Christ, set your hearts on things above, where Christ is, seated at the right hand of God. Set your minds on things above, not on earthly things.
COLOSSIANS 3:1-2 NIV

Social media: an escape, a gift, a communicative tool, a joy stealer, a comparison thief, a comedian, entertainment. Social media can be fun. But it can also become an idol when we don't recognize it as such. Suddenly, instead of opening up the Bible, we are clicking on our phones checking Facebook, posting photos, and updating statuses seeking attention and approval from people rather than our Creator.

God's desire for our life is that we chose him above all else. He wants to be our focal point, one we return to time and again, so we don't ever steer too far off course. Instead of seeking approval from others, we turn our eyes toward the one who loves us most, whose voice is the only one we should hear.

In a busy life of choices, it's important to know your back-up is also your best option—seeking God and choosing life with him.

Where do you choose to spend the majority of your time? What choices could you eliminate to stay centered on Jesus?

Jesus, I choose to listen to your voice, right now. Still my heart, calm my mind, and speak because I am listening. Help me to dwell on what is better. I get wrapped up in menial things and I waste time. Give me strength to switch my thoughts from worthless things to you in all your beauty and goodness.

*"The Father gives me the people who are mine.
Every one of them will come to me,
and I will always accept them."*
JOHN 6:37 NCV

When we live for other voices, we will quickly
become worn out and discouraged. Other people's
expectations for how we should live, act, and be are
sometimes unreachable. There is only one voice that
matters, and it can come in a variety of forms—the
voice of God.

Nothing you do or don't do is going to make God
love you any more or any less. Soak it in, so you can
drown out all the other voices. God tells us that we
are loved, we are cherished, and we have significant
value. We are his beloved, his children, his beautiful
creation. This is the voice that matters.

God's voice is the one to come back to when you feel like you're not enough. He will encourage you and remind you that you are.

> *What are the voices you typically listen to?*
> *Can you ignore them and focus only*
> *on the voice that matters?*

Father, I know there will be a lot of voices in my day. Help me to listen to the ones that matter, and most importantly to listen to yours. Thank you for being the one true voice in my life. Help me to recognize when I am dwelling on the wrong voices and conversations, and bring me back to your Word.

*Your word is a lamp to guide my feet
and a light for my path.*
PSALM 119:105 NLT

There will be opportunities that arise that might be surprising to us. We might suddenly be presented with something that feels kind of terrifying. We view it as an opportunity because we see the benefit in it somewhere along the way. We understand that it could be as much of a gift to our lives as a potentially difficult ride or transition before the gift appears.

Stepping through the unknown takes courage, and courage isn't always available. Through the power of prayer, and wrestling with the opportunity's positives and negatives, hopefully we come to the point where our hearts feel the peace we've been looking for. That makes the task of accepting the opportunity much easier.

Are you facing some big decisions right now? You might not feel brave, but you can trust the peace in your heart. That alone takes courage. This opportunity might be one of the biggest surprises of your life; it's wonderful and scary, but perfect for you.

Have you taken a risk and been pleasantly surprised by the outcome? How do you fully give your trust to God?

Lord, give me courage today. I want you to show me new opportunities and I want to have the confidence to step into them. Thank you for your Word that is a lamp to guide me and a light to show me the right path. Let me see your light this evening and give me clarity as I wake up in the morning.

> *Keep turning your back on every sin,*
> *and make "peace" your life motto.*
> *Practice being at peace with everyone.*
> PSALM 34:14 TPT

Women are emotionally driven. They can be easily swayed by feelings in many situations. And while there are many things that women are strong in, emotions are something they often feel they have little control over.

It is easy to get emotionally entangled in arguments or tense situations. We are naturally curious, and we take great interest in what's going on in others' lives. Oftentimes our curiosity is driven by an honest fascination with people and relationships, but if we are not careful, we can easily cross the fine line into gossip and—for lack of a better term—drama.

We are not only to look for peace, we are to chase after it. When someone comes to you and shares a concerning tidbit about a mutual friend, does judging that person create peace in her life or yours? Or does it only add to an already turbulent situation, and cause you stress in an area where none belonged to you? To pursue peace, we must turn from the desire to gossip, judge, and slander, and instead be kind, loving, and gentle.

> *How can you choose to pursue peace in a relationship instead of being caught up in emotions today?*

Father, thank you that you have created me to care. You want me to listen to other people, to empathize with them, and to share their burdens. Help me not to cross over into gossiping about others or sharing something that's not mine to share. I want to be honoring to you in my care for others.

You gave me life and showed me kindness,
and in your providence watched over my spirit.
JOB 10:12 NIV

Kindness. It's an attribute so important to God
that he listed it among the fruit of the spirit (along
with some other pretty good ones: love, joy, peace,
patience, goodness, faithfulness, gentleness, and
self-control). But what does it really mean? Is it just
being friendly to others? Being nice?

True kindness is defined as being more than that. It's
also being generous and considerate. It's a choice
we make each day. We choose to be generous with
our time and with our funds. We opt to consider
others' feelings before our own.

The Bible talks about kindness quite a lot. Even Job, in his misery, recognized how generous and considerate the Lord was of him. When wave after wave of heartbreak took over Job, he still saw God's kindness.

Are you choosing kindness in your day-to-day life? Are you going beyond just being friendly, and being generous? Look for ways in which you can be considerate of others today.

God, please open my eyes to the needs of others and show me ways to be compassionate and kind.

Trust in the Little Things

Those who know Your name will put their trust in You;
For You, LORD, have not forsaken those who seek You.
PSALM 9:10 NKJV

God has given us a huge gift in his faithful nature. He promises us things and sticks to those promises without fail.

It feels easier to trust God in the big moments, the desperate moments. But what about the everyday moments? The times that we grab hold of control and want to do it all ourselves. In those moments, we can press into him without restraint. Let go, cry out to him, ask him to carry you. And he will. The everyday moments that might feel crooked will be straightened. He will carry you as he promises.

How beautiful is this God! He will give you a path to confidently walk on if all you do is trust him.

Where do you have the most difficulty trusting God? Practice letting go in those moments. Trust him.

God, thank you for being so trustworthy. You have never left me and you have not given up on me. Thank you for carrying me in difficult seasons, and for laughing with me in the good times. I enjoy being with you.

> *"They will be like a tree planted by the water*
> *that sends out its roots by the stream…*
> *and never fails to bear fruit."*
> JEREMIAH 17:8 NIV

Have you ever tried to nurture a plant in a pot? It can flourish with persistent watering, moving it to the right temperature and light, and pruning it when it gets too big. Usually it grows straight up since the pot restricts the roots from growing too wide. Up and up it grows. But if you forget about it for a while, not caring for it the way it was designed to be cared for, it can start to brown, wither, and eventually, it will die.

Roots. They make all the difference in health. Roots take shape underground, where you can't see. Often roots show the true health of anything we examine.

We should have deep roots in our heart's devotion to God. Deep doesn't mean a long history; it means that what happens in our homes, our hearts, and our relationships are nourishing and pleasing to God.

Where is your heart health today, spiritually speaking? Do you need persistent watering and nourishment? Take the time today to ask God for that and watch as your roots come alive.

God, when I feel like I'm getting a little brown or wilted, I want to come to you, my caretaker, and start again. Each time I do, I recognize that my roots grow a little deeper and you make me a little stronger. Thank you for your care of me.

He who dwells in the secret place of the Most High
Shall abide under the shadow of the Almighty.
PSALM 91:1 NKJV

Have you ever been awake when you think no one else is? Maybe you had an early morning flight, and you feel you are the only person who could possibly be stirring at that hour.

It feels kind of magical, doesn't it? It's like you have an unshared secret. Regardless of you being a night owl, morning person, or somewhere in-between, there is peace that comes with meeting Jesus in secret—when your world has stopped for a bit.

Whatever it looks like, rising early or staying up late, taking a work break, a study break, or a mommy break, finding that quiet is where you can actually acquire strength. We need spiritual food to conquer each day.

Can you find daily quiet time to meet with Jesus? He will meet you in that space, filling you with peace, strength, and love to go out and conquer the world.

As I spend a moment reflecting on you, Jesus, help me to remember that this is the lasting part of my day. This is where I gain my strength and hope for all that lies ahead.

By the grace given to me I say to everyone among you not to think of himself more highly than he ought to think, but to think with sober judgment, each according to the measure of faith that God has assigned.

ROMANS 12:3 ESV

Have you ever felt like you were split-second judged? You had an encounter, it didn't go as planned, and immediately you felt less than ideal. We desire grace for ourselves when we are having a "bad day," but it's so easy to forget to extend that same grace to others. Maybe we've done it for so long that we don't even realize we are doing it.

Here is what we need to remember: we are the same. We are children of the Most High God, precious, beautifully made in his image. We belong to Jesus. Let us ask God to give us hearts to see others for who they are, and remember they are nothing less than we are.

Have you had a recent encounter where you've judged someone or haven't extended grace? Reflect on the people in your life and your heart toward them.

God, give me your eyes for other people. Help me to see them as you do. I want to respond with love and grace to others even when they are difficult or mean. Help me not to be judgmental toward those I come across each day but to love them instead.